Ambushed by Glory in My Grief

REBECCA CARPENTER

Cover photography by Rebecca Carpenter.

ISBN: 978-1-941733-85-1

Published by EA Books Publishing a division of
Living Parables of Central Florida, Inc. a 501c3
EABooksPublishing.com

DEDICATION

In memory of

My mom and dad
Marjorie and John Davison

My husband
Alan

ENDORSEMENTS

"To us, and many others, Alan and Becky were "Team Carpenter." When Alan moved to Heaven, Becky began dealing with her grief through beautiful devotional writings. She is living proof that while the pain never gets smaller, God will make it possible for you to grow bigger around it. If you are grieving, Becky's words will help you stay close to God and grow bigger around your pain."

Joel and Becky Hunter
Senior Pastor and wife of Northland-A Church Distributed in Casselberry, FL

"I walked this journey with Rebecca. Her spiritual path is rooted in the Scriptures, reflections, and prayers. The bedrock of these devotionals comes from the depths of her own personal encounters in the Lord and from life and death experiences with family and friends.

Rebecca's expressions of truth with passion in these devotionals come from the overflow of her own healing, recovery, restoration, and the abundant life she has in Christ Jesus. With intense focus and intentionality she takes us into the Word, into her world of pain, pleasure, and observations from nature so that we find rest and joy in our LORD together.

I was a witness to many of the references to her husband Alan. I received mentoring, coaching and insights for living from him for over a decade on our short-term mission trips and church life together. These writings embody and embrace their relationships."

Pastor Gus Davies
Northland-A Church Distributed in Casselberry, FL

"Becky could have easily let self-pity and sorrow overwhelm her after the deaths of both her parents and dearly loved husband. Instead, she opened her eyes and heart to sense God's presence and prompting in nature and everyday circumstances. Thankfully, Becky skillfully penned the insights God revealed to her. What she shares through these personal writings will greatly comfort others as they travel their own grief journey."

Georgia Bruton
Friend and writer, North Carolina

"Rebecca shares her personal journey through grief in this excellent devotional that brings a clear message of hope. A resource for lay individuals, as well as professionals."

Lynda D.W.G. Mason
Minister & Coordinator of Stephen Ministry
at Northland-A Church Distributed in Casselberry, FL
Chaplain and Retired Grief & Trauma Counselor.

"Her path has not been easy having to deal with the multiple losses of loved ones.

And amidst tears and vulnerability there is triumph. This is a must read for those seeking hope and encouragement."

Bill Yearick
Friend and widower, North Carolina

CONTENTS

	Acknowledgments	i
	Introduction	1
Devo 1	Be Thankful? Rejoice Too?	3
Devo 2	Dad's Final Journey	5
Devo 3	God's Perfect Timing	7
Devo 4	The Rest of My Birthday Story	9
Devo 5	A Tearful Shopping Trip	11
Devo 6	Our Christmas Miracles	13
Devo 7	The Way to Heaven	15
Devo 8	A Family's Love	17
Devo 9	Astonishing Gifts	19
Devo 10	The Papers	21
Devo 11	Show at the Lake	23
Devo 12	One More Trial	25
Devo 13	Molly's Awareness	27
Devo 14	A Stray Hair	29
Devo 15	Moving On	31
Devo 16	My Best Encourager Gone	33
Devo 17	An Unforeseen Prayer	35
Devo 18	More Trials and Pain	37
Devo 19	My Easter Crosses	39
Devo 20	Good Friday?	41

Devo 21	Mysterious Gifts	43
Devo 22	Gampa in Heaven	45
Devo 23	Thriving Despite Afflictions	47
Devo 24	Widow's First Anniversary Alone	49
Devo 25	A Granddaughter's Insight	51
Devo 26	Healing from Melon Balls	53
Devo 27	What is Your Rose?	55
Devo 28	Sunshine in the Grief	57
Devo 29	Reminders of Love and Compassion	59
Devo 30	Dark Clouds	61
Devo 31	Unfocused and Jumbled	63
Devo 32	Compassionate Crocheting	65
Devo 33	Sharing Comfort through the Pain	67
Devo 34	Autumn Times	69
Devo 35	Allowing Myself to Trust	71
Devo 36	Dismal to Vibrant	73
Devo 37	Message from a Spider Web	75
Devo 38	Traveling the Bridge	77
Devo 39	Don't Forget	79
Devo 40	Tender Birthday Memories	81
	About the Author	83

ACKNOWLEDGMENTS

For years as I sent my writings to friends and family members, I often heard, "You should write a book." The thought overwhelmed me but I continued filling notebook after notebook.

My parents and husband encouraged me to write and share my stories. After they passed away, their words constantly played in my mind. Friends kept telling me to think about doing a book. Comments came.

"Have you started your book?"

"I print up all of your writings and keep them in a notebook."

"I send your writings to my friends."

"Your writings really touch me."

"I needed that."

"I cried when I read it."

Many people encouraged and inspired me to compile my book. If I started listing names, I am afraid I would forget someone. Anyone who responded to something I wrote, encouraged me to keep going.

As I began healing, it was time to publish a book that could help comfort others facing their own grief.

Thank you to all of my encouragers.

Introduction

For years, inspiration for my devotionals came from wildlife, bodies of water, flowers, sunsets, and children. But numerous difficult life circumstances changed that. First, Mother's already fragile health declined. Next, doctors diagnosed my husband, Alan, with idiopathic pulmonary fibrosis, which shook our world. Finally, my dad's body could no longer overcome serious health issues. Three of those I loved most faced death at the same time.

As stress and anxiety grew, writing provided a positive outlet. Throughout doctor visits, hospital stays, financial paperwork, hospice care, memorial services, and unending grief, pain blended with touches of joy. When I shared my devotionals online during that time, I learned that my words comforted and encouraged others. Family members, friends, and even strangers cried with me in my pain and rejoiced in the blessings.

As God led me to write, I knew His plan was for me to share my journey. He had certainly given me plenty of material to write about and guidance in writing. Often, I had no idea what to share, but when I prayed, the words flowed. Sometimes, I resisted putting my thoughts on paper, but not for long. God's gentle prodding reminded me that someone needed words of comfort. Perhaps, I wrote only for myself, or maybe someone else had a trial I knew nothing about. Even on my darkest days, I received glimmers of hope. When the time was right, after gradual healing and much encouragement, I selected forty of my devotionals that illustrate how I dealt with the grief of losing three loved ones in eleven months.

Several significant situations in the Bible lasted forty days. Noah and his family endured uncertainty and apprehension in the ark while it rained for forty days. Moses fasted and waited on Mt. Sinai for forty days before God gave him the stone tablets inscribed with the Ten Commandments. After he smashed the tablets when the people disobeyed God, Moses returned to the mountain for forty more days of fasting and waiting before God again provided instructions for their lives. After His baptism, Jesus fasted and was tempted by Satan in the desert for forty days. Following His resurrection, Jesus remained for forty days to meet with his disciples and prepare them for their future.

My hope is that wherever you are in your grief, which comes from many difficult situations, the Lord will strengthen and inspire you as He did for me when I needed it the most. The fog of grief confuses and insulates, but God breaks through with touches of glory. Even though each person's journey is unique, if a family member or friend is grieving, this book can help you understand the mixed-up world of grief so you can be more supportive and understanding. Hopefully, the writings will allow you to see how God's love, peace, and grace helped me endure pain, uncertainty, and loneliness just as He did for those in the Bible long ago.

He continues to encourage and offer guidance for whatever lies ahead. Time lessened my sorrow, but it remains woven into my life. Along with the continued ambushes of grief, I am also thankful to be ambushed by glory.

Devo 1

Be Thankful? Rejoice Too?

Rejoice always. Pray without ceasing. In everything give thanks, for this is the will of God in Christ Jesus toward you. Don't quench the Spirit. (1 Thessalonians 5:16-19 WEB)

Rejoice is all circumstances? How could I do that with all the problems in my family? For months and months, one trial after another hit us.

Some days, I wondered how I would survive, but God always gave me just what I needed. The passage above, from 1 Thessalonians 5, reminded me to be thankful in everything. When I focused on the blessings, even small ones, instead of the trials, thankfulness became easier.

We're praying for you.
Let us know if there is anything we can do.
We are lifting you and your family up in prayer.

From around the world, family members and friends sent words of comfort. Hundreds of people prayed. In the midst of continuing trials, God used His people to provide encouragement and hope in numerous ways.

At my husband's appointment with his pulmonologist, my tears flowed when Alan told the staff about my parents' illnesses. A nurse took my hand and said she would be praying. The receptionist left her computer to give me a hug. I felt lighter when I left the office.

At Mother's rehab facility, one therapist asked how Dad was doing after his first stroke. Her eyes told me she really cared. Down the hallway, another worker asked how things were going. When I said it was hard, tears gushed again. Instead of hurrying back to her job, she stopped and squeezed my hand. Our brief encounter showed her concern and bolstered my spirit.

When my dad's prognosis was extremely grave, I received support and encouragement in unexpected ways. A respiratory nurse who helped revive my dad after his cardiac arrest made sure she found my family to tell us she was praying. Two hospital chaplains, one a friend of my brother's and the other, who played softball with my dad, each took time out of their busy day to pray with us. As I waited for the hospital elevator, two volunteers exited with a cart of coffee, tea, and sweets. They smiled, handed me a cookie, and wished me a great day. Holding a cheery sunflower, a friend joined me on my patio. Her hug and visit revived me after a tiring day of hospital visits. Ducks skimmed the lake, birds chirped merrily, and a gentle breeze rustled the leaves, furnishing a place of serenity during my numerous trials. Even during pain and tribulation, I learned it is possible to give thanks and be joyful.

Heavenly Father, thank you for your blessings that come within the trials. Amen.

Devo 2

Dad's Final Journey

May you all continue the journey with your spirits strengthened by the grace of the Lord Jesus, the Anointed One. [Amen.] (Philippians 4:23 VOICE)

After almost eighty-nine years, Dad neared the end of his earthly journey. Only after Mother assured him she would be fine did he make the difficult decision to forgo additional treatment for his spreading cancer. The following day, he joined Mother in hospice care.

In less than a week, his condition deteriorated quickly. A second stroke robbed him of his speech. A wheelchair replaced his legs. He had no appetite. For a strong athlete who had played softball only a few months earlier, the change was dramatic.

His independence and stubbornness often caused him to be a less than ideal patient. However, for years those same characteristics kept him from giving up when he faced many heart issues, cancer, and multiple surgeries.

Thankfully, one evening a miracle occurred. In their side-by-side wheelchairs, Dad and Mother watched the Kentucky Derby and ate grilled hamburgers with my brother Ken and his family. The news gave me hope that he was improving.

That evening he returned to his bed and limited lifestyle. From then on, he only spoke a few words.

On my next visit, I took his hand and told him that I loved him. He smiled, looked into my eyes, and said clearly, "I love you too."

With all the struggles he endured, I thought he could overcome the latest ones too. For years, he cared for Mother as she fought leukemia, diabetes, and other health issues. He had been the strong one.

Our family attended his basketball games, track events, and softball games after he retired. Medals lined the walls of his garage. He continued playing even when there were no other players his age. He realized his skills had declined and talked of quitting. But the younger players said he inspired them. Would his determination pull him through again?

Each day I waited. Then, soon after my visit, the dreaded phone call came one morning. Dad had passed away peacefully with Mother and my brother Joe by his side.

I never thought Dad's journey would end first. Alan comforted me in my sadness. I grieved not only because of losing my dad but also because of Mother's terminal illness and impending death (not to mention Alan's). How could I endure more pain?

The miracle of Dad's special night reminded me of God's care and blessings. I knew He would be with me throughout my own journey of grief.

Heavenly Father, thank you for my earthly father, who inspired and encouraged me. Thank you for walking beside me. Amen.

Devo 3

God's Perfect Timing

"For I know the plans I have for you," declares the Lord, "plans to prosper you and not to harm you, plans to give you hope and a future. then you will seek me and find me when you seek me with all your heart." (Jeremiah 29: 11-12 NIV)

Because of Alan's progressing idiopathic pulmonary fibrosis, he suggested we downsize from our large home to a smaller one so it would be easier for me when he was gone. Even though I knew he was right, I hated the reason for the move. We visited many retirement communities and finally decided to build a more manageable home in an active adult community.

Soon after we made the commitment, Mother's health declined and then surprisingly, so did my dad's. For months, we dealt with hospitals, surgeries, rehab centers, hospice, and then my dad's death, which kept my life in turmoil. With an already overwhelmed life, I couldn't handle one more thing. Alan kindly agreed that listing our home could be put on hold for a while.

But as cement blocks rose from the sandy lot of our new home, I knew we had to sell our bigger one. Reluctantly, because I knew there would be added stress with keeping it ready for prospective buyers, I agreed to put our home on the market. Several people, including realtors, showed up and thought it was a beautiful house, but no one made an offer. For weeks, nobody came at all. When I worried about the lack of buyers, Alan remained unruffled. "It's all in God's timing," he said over and over.

The thought of getting rid of furniture, disposing of mementos, packing, and actually moving overwhelmed me. But the expenses for two houses distressed me too. Alan's constant assurances calmed me. Numerous friends joined us in prayer. Alan and I asked God for the right buyer, at the right time, and for the right price.

We waited and waited for the right buyers. After the roof appeared on our new home and workers added details inside, our realtor called about a showing. After their third visit, a couple made an offer. Within two weeks, a contract was signed.

Prayers had been answered. God knew the right time since I could not have handled a move along with my parents' illnesses, Dad's death, and dealing with their estate. When situations stabilized somewhat, our home sold. By then my life had become a little more normal. Our new house was almost completed. The time between closing dates gave us plenty of time for a leisurely move. The price wasn't too far from our asking price. Alan was right all along. God knew the perfect time.

Loving Father, thank you for answering my prayers at the right time according to your plan. Give me patience to wait and not worry. Amen.

Devo 4

The Rest of My Birthday Story

Grace to you and peace from God our Father and the Lord Jesus Christ. Blessed be the God and Father of our Lord Jesus Christ, the Father of mercies and God of all comfort; who comforteth us in all our affliction, that we may be able to comfort them that are in any affliction, through the comfort wherewith we ourselves are comforted of God. (2 Corinthians 1:2-4 ASV)

When we got up, Alan didn't even mention my birthday as he always had done. When I talked to my mom that morning, I had to remind her what day it was. It was my first birthday without Dad. No one had called to wish me a special day.

During my private pity party, tears flowed. I grieved for the normal life I no longer had. As I sat on the patio peering at the lake through blurry eyes, the phone rang. My good friend Sallie shared my pain as we talked, laughed, and cried.

After the phone call ended, I stepped into the house.

"Happy birthday," Alan said. "I planned to tell you earlier when I first woke up, but I was so focused on being able to breathe." Even with his progressing lung disease, he hadn't forgotten.

Later in the day when I called mother again, she didn't recall our earlier conversation. Right away she said, "Happy birthday." She remembered my birthday too.

A number of thoughtful friends and family members cheered me up with birthday cards, phone calls, e-mail messages, and hugs.

For dinner, Alan took me to a local award-winning restaurant. A welcome card with our name and glittery confetti decorated our table. We savored our delicious meal and thoroughly enjoyed our time together.

The following day, my son, Chris, and his wife, Anne, prepared a special birthday dinner. My three young granddaughters decorated their dining room for the celebration. Each youngster made me a beautiful card. Though he was weak and tired, Alan, tethered to his oxygen tank, joined my birthday celebration.

Special, loving gifts reminded me that even though my day began with sadness, I didn't remain there. Alan rested for the entire day so we could go out for our unforgettable dinner. Family members and friends cheered me up and made sure I wasn't forgotten. Every prayer and kind gesture comforted me. Even during a distressing period of time, it was a joyful, memorable occasion.

Dear Lord, thank you for those who comfort me. You are the ultimate Comforter. Amen.

Devo 5

A Tearful Shopping Trip

"He will wipe away from them every tear from their eyes. Death will be no more; neither will there be mourning, nor crying, nor pain, any more. The first things have passed away." (Revelation 21:4 WEB)

Jingle bells rang. Festive trees sparkled. Christmas music blared overhead. Families laughed and filled shopping carts. I tried to ignore the colorful decorations and cheerful people. At the first store, I focused on finding perfect gifts for my mom, whose terminal illness kept her housebound. I roamed from aisle to aisle but nothing I saw seemed right for her. Everything was the wrong color, size, or style. While traveling from one store to another, tears threatened to explode.

With each clerk's jovial greeting, "How are you today?" I mumbled, "OK."

What if I told them the real story? Would they hear me if I told them my dad had died a few months earlier and my mother was terminally ill? Would they care if I said doctors had given my husband six months to live? Finally, tired and discouraged, I retreated to the solitude of my car. When the engine started so did my tears.

I desperately longed for the happiness of previous Christmases. Savoring Mother's cooking at my parents' home. Opening gifts with the whole family looking on. Mother, Dad, and Alan all robust, healthy, and able to fully enjoy the Christmas celebration.

Grief grabbed me like a stealthy intruder. Unexpected and unwelcome. I mourned the loss of my dad. My heart broke at the impending deaths of my mother and husband. Thinking about family and friends who would also face empty or nearly empty chairs at their holiday tables filled me with more sadness. In spite of the tears, I fondly remembered happier times and the true reason for Christmas—to celebrate the birth of Jesus.

The adorable baby Jesus pictured on Christmas cards grew up into a life filled with pain, trials and hardships. He experienced sorrow and wept over losses too. His followers suffered grief when He was imprisoned, crucified, and died. But joy returned on Easter at His resurrection. Remembering his turbulent and often disturbing life on earth helped me cope with my own despair and suffering.

In this world, grief and sorrow blend with joy and happiness. Life on earth is not the end of the story for those who believe in Jesus. Only in heaven will there be no pain or sorrow.

Heavenly Father, with your presence comfort those who grieve. Give gifts of peace, joy, and contentment. Amen.

Devo 6

Our Christmas Miracles

*May God be merciful to us, bless us, and cause his face
to shine on us.* (Psalm 67:1 WEB)

In the blackness before dawn, Alan and I loaded our car and headed out. For several years, we joined my son, Chris, and his family on Christmas morning. However, with Alan's progressing pulmonary fibrosis, we weren't sure if he would be able to go. Surprisingly, his improved breathing that morning allowed him to leave his oxygen tank in the car.

Christmas lights sparkled from the roof when we drove up to Chris and Anne's home. They whispered a welcome. We added our gifts to the piles under the glittering tree but saw no excited granddaughters.

After a few minutes, Ashlyn and Emily bounded out of their room. Three-year-old Molly clung to her dad's shoulder and stared at us through droopy eyes. Within a short time, festive paper littered the floor. Giggles and squeals of delight accompanied Christmas music. We opened gifts and learned new games. Enthusiastic girls bounced on a new trampoline. After the festivities, we enjoyed a delicious brunch.

Later in the morning, we drove to our second celebration at my brother and sister-in-law's home. Enticing aromas and a glittering tree welcomed us as our extended family gathered for a joyful meal. With mother's declining health, we didn't know if she would feel like joining the celebration. While the other adults sat in the dining room, mother's caregiver wheeled her to the kitchen table where the five great grandchildren and I joined her for our holiday meal. Their antics kept us smiling and free from tears because of Dad's empty chair. She beamed and relished her time out of bed with her family. God's beautiful miracle lifted our spirits.

Alan received additional miracles. For weeks, medication had taken away his ability to taste food. But that day he savored each delicious bite. He piled food high on his plate and returned for seconds before indulging in desserts.

With no scary hoses or hissing noises, Molly and Emily jumped into Alan's lap. Molly, who loved to climb in his lap, had stayed away when oxygen tubes wrapped his face. His arms hugged both girls. All three of them laughed and made silly faces. Even without using his oxygen, he remained strong the entire day.

The playfulness of children brought joy that day as we grieved the loss of my dad. We knew it would probably be the last Christmas celebration with Alan and Mother.

As our family anticipated a difficult time, God orchestrated a series of small miracles, which contributed to our blessed Christmas.

At the end of the day, mother still couldn't walk as leukemia weakened her. Alan required oxygen to breathe because of pulmonary fibrosis. Dad didn't return to us. But we rejoiced and were thankful for our Christmas miracles.

Gracious Father, thank you for each miracle — even the small ones. Amen.

Devo 7

The Way to Heaven

"Have I not commanded you? Be strong and courageous. Do not be terrified; do not be discouraged, for the Lord your God will be with you wherever you go." (Joshua 1:9 NIV)

Though tethered to an oxygen line the last few months of life, Alan's spirit remained strong as his body weakened. When he wasn't too exhausted, he loved sharing God's words with visitors and made phone calls to those who were far away. He prayed for wisdom before each conversation and asked the Holy Spirit for the right words each person needed to hear. He delivered short, but powerful messages. Peace about his upcoming death never wavered. Even when he reminisced about days when he played racquetball and lifted heavy weights at the gym, he didn't complain or get angry about his debilitating disease. He reminded me it was all part of God's plan and was thankful for the blessings he had received.

One day, even though he had little strength, he insisted my small Bible study group meet at our house. In spite of a raspy voice and shortness of breath, he shared his love of Jesus with my friends. His outward body was wasting away, but joy radiated the love of Christ to us with his smile and passionate words.

15

A few hours later when he struggled to breathe, he called the hospice nurse. She made an extra visit and showed me how to give him additional medication to aid his breathing, which was more laborious than normal.

That evening I noticed Alan's low oxygen level. "You frightened me," I said.

He looked into my eyes. "Don't be afraid or discouraged. The Lord is with you always. I love you." Then he turned over and went to sleep.

That image etched itself forever in my mind because it was the last time I saw him alive. His passing that night had come as a complete shock to us all.

Don't be afraid or discouraged. The Lord is with you always. I love you.

Those words played over and over like a nonstop recording. How comforting they were as I shared our special time with family and friends. His final words reflected his deep faith and reassured me that God would be with me during my time of grief and throughout my new life as a widow. The peace he received from Jesus enveloped me when I felt as if my life was falling apart. The graceful way he died provided a memorable gift to all who knew him.

Father, thank you for giving peace in the midst of pain and trials. Amen.

Devo 8

A Family's Love

Even a child maketh himself known by his doings,
Whether his work be pure, and whether it be right.
(Proverbs 20:11 ASV)

Mother's in the hospital again.
Dad had a stroke.
We don't know if Mother will make it this time. She's on a respirator.
Dad had cardiac arrest and is on a respirator.
If you want to see Dad one last time, you should come.
Mother probably won't be here much longer.

Every time I called Chris and Anne, because of a family crisis, they responded quickly. For several years, there was one emergency after another as we dealt with diseases, accidents, surgeries, and death.

Sometimes the whole family came, but at other times, Chris arrived alone while Anne kept things going at home. Each problem brought changes to their routines, but they always found a way to help.

Every call was difficult, but the most distressing one came when I was alone in the blackness of night. "Alan is gone," said a voice that sounded like mine.

"I'll be there. Are you OK?" Chris asked.

He soon arrived to help me navigate the initial fog of grief. As I said good-bye to Alan, prepared for his service, and tried to accept that he was really gone, Chris took much of the burden and made sure I was doing OK. He and Anne showed up often with the girls to give me comfort and a brief respite from the pain. We went to Blue Spring Park for a picnic to get out of the house. They invited me to join them on a school field trip to Williamsburg, Virginia, so that I wouldn't be home alone. And Chris checked on me through frequent phone calls and text messages.

Late one night, my phone rang.

"Mom, you need to get to bed."

"How did you know I was up?"

"You were on Facebook."

"I guess I should only send e-mails when I'm up too late." I laughed.

My son's care and concern helped fill my emptiness. He urged me to take care of myself. Planning Alan's memorial service was easier because he and Pastor Gus took care of most details. Alan's legacy showed up in the memorable video Chris created. His heartfelt eulogy showed the bond he had for his stepfather and warmed my grieving heart.

He and Anne opened their home to me whenever I needed a respite. They welcomed me and helped mend my broken heart by including me in their family. As I began to navigate life as a lonely widow, the presence of their family helped dry my tears and eased my grief. They enfolded me in love and strengthened me during my long and grueling journey.

Lord, thank you for the love and support of children and grandchildren. Amen.

Devo 9

Astonishing Gifts

Rejoice in the Lord always: again I will say, Rejoice. Let your forbearance be known unto all men. The Lord is at hand. In nothing be anxious; but in everything by prayer and supplication with thanksgiving let your requests be made known unto God. And the peace of God, which passeth all understanding, shall guard your hearts and your thoughts in Christ Jesus. (Philippians 4:4-7 ASV)

Many years ago, Alan appeared at my door dressed in a pale yellow shirt to match the dozen yellow roses clutched in his hands. I opened the door and heard, "Happy birthday to you."
What a lovely surprise before my special birthday dinner at Disney. As we dated, his thoughtfulness made me love him more and more. During our courtship, he continued to surprise me with bouquets because he knew I loved flowers. However, after our marriage, they didn't come as often.

When pulmonary fibrosis attacked his body and the doctor gave him only six months to live, Alan began preparing me for his death. He made a list to make sure he had everything in order. One item on his list was to keep fresh flowers in the house. As he completed his tasks, we looked for flowers at the grocery store, but none satisfied us. He wanted to find a florist in town, but his energy dwindled and time ran out. There were no fresh flowers at home the night he died. However, the day after he left for heaven a friend surprised me with a pot of delicate pink tulips.

Before dawn two days later, I opened the front door to pick up the newspaper. The porch light spotlighted three lovely white roses in a vase by my door. In amazement, I searched for a card but there was none. With tears streaming down my face, I picked up the vase and lovingly placed it on our kitchen counter. I never found out who left them, but it didn't matter. Someone decided to comfort me with delicate flowers. The following day a long package arrived at my door. When I opened it, a dozen beautiful white roses touched my heart as more tears flowed.

Alan's time and energy ran out before he could satisfy his wish for fresh bouquets. Even though I had not shared our conversation about the flowers, other people fulfilled his plan. God provided comfort for me through friends and family members. Those experiences reminded me that He will continue to give me what I need.

Heavenly Father, thank you for meeting my needs in unexpected ways. Amen.

Devo 10

The Papers

Jehovah is nigh unto them that are of a broken heart,
And saveth such as are of a contrite spirit. (Psalm 34:18
ASV)

The security guard smiled when I walked into the room. I took my number, found a seat, and waited. An elderly couple sat on one side of me and a middle-aged lady on the other. No one spoke or even made eye contact.

A young couple sat behind me. His incessant talking made up for the silence of those beside me. He complained and didn't say one kind word. Their baby rested quietly in a small seat while they verbally attacked each other. Their arguments annoyed me. I wanted to jump up and shout at them to stop. Be thankful for your child. Appreciate each other. I had no patience with selfish, petty behavior.

Before I could chastise them, a lady called my number. I sat down at her window and pulled out my paperwork.

"How may I help you?" the worker asked.

All I could muster was, "My husband passed away." I slid my pile of papers across the counter to her. Tears cracked my voice. She seemed to understand my difficulty.

I tried to compose myself as she carefully examined the papers: a marriage license, a death certificate, and a driver's license. They represented deaths. The death certificate recorded the end of a special life. The marriage license, no longer valid with one partner missing, symbolized the loss of a loving relationship. The void driver's license meant the end of a vigorous man. The process of presenting and examining the required papers in a government office seemed so cold, harsh, and depressing. Alan's vibrant life had been reduced to three documents.

While she worked on her computer, the kind lady silently passed a box of tissues across the desk to me. "Take it one day at a time," she told me. Her compassion and solemn face told me she cared.

I could only nod. In a roomful of people, I felt so alone. I blinked hard to stop the tears.

However, in my car, grief overtook me. With my head on the steering wheel, I sobbed. Finally, when tears slowed to a trickle, I started the car and drove on.

Life wasn't over even though it felt like it. I knew I would have to move on too. In my mixed-up world, God enfolded me and told me I would heal—eventually. He sent family, friends, and even strangers to console and encourage me. Each act of kindness made the journey a little easier. I continued to endure pain, cling to memories, and rest in God's care.

Loving Father, hold me close and heal my wounds. Amen.

Devo 11

Show at the Lake

And I heard a great voice out of the throne saying, Behold, the tabernacle of God is with men, and he shall dwell with them, and they shall be his peoples, and God himself shall be with them, and be their God: and he shall wipe away every tear from their eyes; and death shall be no more; neither shall there be mourning, nor crying, nor pain, any more: the first things are passed away. And he that sitteth on the throne said, Behold, I make all things new. And he saith, Write: for these words are faithful and true. (Revelation 21:3-5 ASV)

Mist swirled over the lake like a troupe of graceful ballerinas. Raindrops dimpled the dark water and formed massive bubbles that erupted over the lake. The deepening slate sky blocked out the dawn's light. Cold damaged grass had turned dismal brown from a once brilliant emerald. Recently vibrant, firm water plants along the bank leaned over in forlorn yellowish-brown masses. Despite the gloominess and frigid chill of the morning, a sense of peace and joy swaddled me with love and contentment.

Wrapped tightly in my fuzzy robe and velour blanket, I experienced a delightful transformation as the morning came alive outside my patio retreat. Tiny birds hopped on the bare branches of dormant cypress trees by the shore. Gentle rain pattered rhythms on the roof. Chirping birds ventured out into the shower. A golden female cardinal perched briefly in the small oak tree near my patio and surveyed the lake. Dancing clouds on the lake twirled in all directions. The filmy ballerinas skipped, whirled, and swayed with exuberance. Though I couldn't run out to touch or catch them, I knew they were real and not only in my imagination.

Their translucent but remarkable appearance reminded me of Alan. No longer could I grasp his hand or embrace him in a loving hug. But his spirit lives on in his legacy of kindness, service, and love for those who knew him. In heaven with a new body free of idiopathic pulmonary fibrosis, he can move easily and breathe freely.

Like the words of the song "I Can Only Imagine," I don't know for sure what he is doing. But I can imagine that he is rejoicing with Jesus which gives me peace and comfort.

Lord, thank you for providing comfort and peace to those who are left behind when loved ones come to you. Amen.

Devo 12

One More Trial

When I am afraid, I will put my trust in you. In God, I praise his word. In God, I put my trust. I will not be afraid. What can flesh do to me? (Psalm 56:3-4 WEB)

With Alan's death so fresh, I couldn't believe my family faced another challenge. My daughter-in-law, Anne, called to let me know Chris, had driven himself from work to the emergency room because of chest pains. With anxious thoughts, I wondered what would happen next.

Immediately, my mothering instinct kicked in. I threw some clothes into a bag. Then I grabbed the meat, salad, and dessert I had planned to serve Chris and his family for dinner that night at my house. For thirty minutes, I prayed and prayed during my drive to their home.

While I watched my three granddaughters, Anne drove to the hospital and stayed with Chris as he endured test after test. The doctors kept him overnight for observation. Finally, the hospital released him the following day. Thankfully, nothing abnormal showed up.

After a restless and mostly sleepless night, I returned home exhausted and ready for a nap. When I went to my door, I noticed a shoebox wrapped in brown paper on my porch. There was no name from the sender but only a Post Office Box number, city, and state. I cut the tape that held the box securely, pulled off the lid, and peered inside. A carefully written message nestled on top of the tissue paper wrapping.

> *Just a simple prayer shawl*
> *Knit with prayers of love and comfort for you*
> *To cover you with blessings*
> *For the times you are going through.*
> *I pray that wrapped around you*
> *You will feel our Savior's arms*
> *Holding you and loving you*
> *And keeping you safe and warm.*
> *Blessed be the God and Father of our Lord Jesus Christ,*
> *the Father of mercies and God of all comfort;*
> (2 Corinthians 1:3 ASV)

Beneath the wrappings lay a lovely beige prayer shawl. The knitted symbol of God's love hugged me when I wrapped it around my shoulders. The love of a compassionate yet unknown knitter warmed my heart at the perfect time. Frequently, Alan told me he was ready to see Jesus. Though he knew it would be hard for me, he felt confident I would be strong and supported by family and friends. He was right. Over and over blessings and support came to comfort and strengthen me.

Loving Father, thank you for good medical reports and for caring people who reach out to the hurting. Amen.

Devo 13

Molly's Awareness

Know this: children are a gift from the Eternal... (Psalm 127: 3 VOICE)

May you have the privilege of seeing your grandchildren as they grow....(Psalm 128: 6 VOICE)

Only a few weeks after my husband's death, I traveled to Williamsburg, Virginia, with my son and his family because they didn't want me to be home alone so soon. Ashlyn's fourth-grade family field trip gave us all an opportunity to get away from the stresses we faced with Alan's passing.

Before the trip, I continued my tradition of gathering small gifts for each of my three young granddaughters to keep them occupied during the long hours on the road. They always looked forward to unwrapping their numbered presents at intervals during each trip. The two older girls had learned to handle waiting between each gift. They sat in the third seat of the van contentedly playing games, reading, and writing.

Three-year-old Molly looked forward to every gift, but she wanted to open them one after the other. Since I sat next to her in the second row of seats, I tried to keep her busy. We talked about all sorts of things. We played many of her games and read books over and over until her mother said it was time to open another gift.

With enthusiasm she tore the paper off of present number five. Without a word to anyone, she grabbed a pen in her tiny hand, put her head down, and began drawing on the colorful notepad. For a few minutes, she concentrated on each detail before holding it up for us to see her creation. Then she announced, "This is Mommy's sad face when Grandpa died."

Anne and I looked at each other in surprise and then at the simple, sad face on the paper. No one in the car had been talking about Alan even though I had definitely been thinking about him. He must have been on Molly's mind too. Though very young, she noticed and processed more about death and feelings than we ever imagined.

"We were sad when Grandpa died," I told her, "because we miss him. But we know he's with Jesus."

Molly nodded and without a word returned to her next drawing.

Her actions showed me that children can guide us as we deal with the hard parts of life. She acknowledged the pain of loss but didn't dwell on it. Then she confidently went on with life.

Father, help me be more like a child in trusting you for whatever lies ahead. Amen.

Devo 14

A Stray Hair

Oh satisfy us in the morning with thy lovingkindness, that we may rejoice and be glad all our days. (Psalm 90:14 ASV)

A single hair glistened on the lampshade. Carefully, I pulled it off and held it like a precious gem in my hand. *Should I keep it?* A few weeks ago, the hair would have been in the garbage without a thought. But since that time, my life changed dramatically.

The wavy silver hair wasn't mine. Memories of Alan bombarded me as I stared at the ringlet that made me smile. While he relaxed on our couch watching television, I gave him hundreds of head rubs. When pulmonary fibrosis attacked his body, he rested more often and received more head massages. I giggled each time he told me that the silver strands were actually his younger shade of blonde.

Multiple times I cut his thick, wavy locks. How scared I was of messing up when he first asked me to be his barber before we were married. At that time, he sported a military-type flat top. Later, his style lengthened and I grew more confident with the scissors and razor. Over the years, his hair thinned, and a sparse spot on his crown became a challenge to hide. Barbering sessions gave us time to talk and laugh.

Only a couple of weeks before he died, he sat in a white plastic chair in the driveway of our new home as I clipped. Without needing his oxygen, he enjoyed talking to neighbors who stopped to chat. The balmy weather delighted us, and neither of us realized it would be his last haircut. Though tears threatened to spill, pleasant memories pushed them away. Finally, the stray hair went into the trash. I didn't need it to remember special memories with Alan.

During the last months of his life, we spent hours talking and sharing our thoughts. Alan shared final words and his faith with many people who phoned or came to visit. With limited energy, he delivered short but powerful sermons. He told everyone to live each day as though it was your last because it might be. Cherish your loved ones. Make special memories. Don't put important things off. Be thankful for what God has given to you. His advice continues to comfort me as I live my life without him.

Father, thank you for each day. Help me to appreciate all you have given to me. Amen.

Devo 15

Moving On

Grace to you and peace from God our Father and the Lord Jesus Christ.

Blessed be the God and Father of our Lord Jesus Christ, the Father of mercies and God of all comfort; who comforts us in all our affliction, that we may be able to comfort those who are in any affliction, through the comfort with which we ourselves are comforted by God.
(2 Corinthians 1:2-4 WEB)

A tiny patch of rose glowed between the pines. Within seconds, an invisible paintbrush tinted the eastern sky with shades of pink and blue. A ball of fire blazed behind the forest along the shoreline. Reflections of trees, clouds, and the sun shimmered on the dark lake. Birds twittered and sang.

As I watched the spectacular display, I thought of the recent deaths of Alan and my dad. The sunrise soothed me in my pain. It offered hope and comfort for my continuing journey without them. *Do they see my sunrise? Are they watching me?*

Gradually, the clouds dissipated. A yellowish-white glow replaced the pink and blue in the ever-changing sky. Each palette of colors produced a unique but charming picture.

My life was constantly changing too. Loved ones and friends came and went. Moves required making new friends. Bodies weakened. Little stayed the same. I couldn't stop the progression of life. If I resisted and desperately tried to hang onto the past, I'd be miserable. I had to choose to accept and adapt to my new life so I could move on.

Even as he was dying, Alan prepared me for life without him. I wanted to pretend he would get better. He persisted. We went through files together. He updated accounts to remove his name. He gave away some of his clothes and special mementos. The process often pained me but also comforted me because his wishes were being carried out. He wanted to make life as easy as he could for me after he was gone.

Along the same lines, Dad listed all of my parents' accounts, passwords, and important phone numbers. He wanted it to be easier for me when I had to handle their affairs. At first, I didn't even want to look at the folder he gave me. When I became the trustee, how thankful I was for his preparation.

Alan didn't want me to dwell on his death but to continue living and serving. Every day I think of him and my dad. They touched many lives as they loved and served others. Both left a legacy that remains a vital part of my life and to those who knew them.

Loving Father, thank you for those you put in my life who nurture and love me. Help me to spread their legacies as I move on. Amen.

Devo 16

My Best Encourager Gone

Rejoice with those who rejoice. Weep with those who weep. Be of the same mind one toward another. Don't set your mind on high things, but associate with the humble. Don't be wise in your own conceits. (Romans 12:15-16 WEB)

"I don't know how you do it," Alan often said after reading one of my writings. "Your work touches thousands of people around the world as you send them out on the Internet. You have no idea how many."

He encouraged me to attend the Florida Christian Writers Conference even though his health was declining. I didn't feel comfortable leaving him alone, but he insisted. Only because he wanted me to go did I register for the conference, which was an hour's drive away. A few weeks before the conference, he passed away. With such a fresh loss, I requested a refund. I felt concentration would be difficult. Crying around so many people would make me uncomfortable.

"Of course we'll refund your money," the president told me. "But think about coming so we can love on you."

I told her I would think about it but didn't believe I could handle being there. As the deadline approached, I remembered my best encourager's words. Alan's desire for me to go changed my mind. I packed my bags and drove alone down country roads to the retreat center.

What a blessing it was! Those who knew the situation welcomed me with open arms. During morning devotions, singing, listening to speakers, watching the film *Unconditional*, or in conversation, my tears flowed often but didn't linger. Each teardrop brought kind words, prayers, and hugs. Many shared their own struggles and heartaches. I wasn't alone.

The conference brought God's people together to share His love through writing. Whether a best-selling author, national speaker, screenwriter, photographer, or a first timer like me, we all shared in God's love.

Everyone amazed me with their helpfulness and compassion towards each other. We offered prayers, celebrated writing victories, and made donations to special causes. No one elevated themselves above anyone else, but everyone encouraged others.

I went home ready to write more of Alan's story to inspire others. Knowledge and suggestions from the retreat jammed my head. Thankfulness filled my heart. I looked forward to God's plan for me as I traveled my journey of grief. Even though my chief supporter left my side, his memory pushed me forward. Fellow writers motivated and uplifted me. God provided just what I needed.

Father, thank you for the people you put in my life. Both those who have gone to be with You and those who are still with me. Amen.

Devo 17

An Unforeseen Prayer

In the same way, the Spirit also helps our weaknesses, for we don't know how to pray as we ought. But the Spirit himself makes intercession for us with groanings which can't be uttered. He who searches the hearts knows what is on the Spirit's mind, because he makes intercession for the saints according to God. (Romans 8:26-27 WEB)

The small local pharmacy fit the image of small-town America. A lone customer and clerk chatted like old friends, which they probably were. Quite a contrast to the chain stores I normally frequented.

Tax time had taken me to the store for a list of my dad's prescriptions. Another reminder that he was gone. For days I searched for information needed to file my parents' tax return.

Dad always took care of their returns, but when he passed away, the responsibility became mine. Mother's declining health prevented her from assisting me. The insurance company refused to give me information about his medications because they didn't recognize my position as trustee of his estate.

Thankfully, their local pharmacy offered a printout of the medications they had provided. After the assistant handed me the paper, the pharmacist walked up to the counter.

"I'm so sorry for what your family has gone through this year. I think about you and your mom a lot." His solemn face expressed his sorrow. "Your parents used to come in frequently. They were sweet people. How is she doing?"

"Not good. She's very weak," I said. "Besides losing my dad, my husband died recently."

He shook his head. "I'm sorry."

While we talked, I noticed the clerk standing nearby. Tears filled her eyes. I thanked the pharmacist for his help and turned to leave.

When I was a few steps from the door, the clerk caught up with me. "I just felt the urge to pray for you," she told me. "Would that be OK?"

"That would be good." I smiled.

"I don't usually do this but felt God telling me to pray with you."

Her short prayer gave me courage and strength.

"I'll keep praying for you and your family," she said.

"Thank you. Prayers have gotten us through all of this."

I left the store with a lighter step. Unexpected compassion and a simple prayer helped me face the difficult tasks ahead as trustee for my dad and Alan. Her boldness in praying for a stranger spoke to my heart. How many times had I felt the urge to pray or offer comfort to someone but ignored it because I wasn't sure how it would be received? Her heartfelt gesture and obedience gave me a gift that God knew I needed right then. Hopefully, the Holy Spirit's promptings will lead me to offer comfort and encouragement with greater boldness.

Father, thank you for the prayers of your people, even those from strangers. Amen.

Devo 18

More Trials and Pain

Then shall the virgin rejoice in the dance, and the young men and the old together; for I will turn their mourning into joy, and will comfort them, and make them rejoice from their sorrow. (Jeremiah 31:13 ASV)

After enduring over a year of turmoil and grief, I wondered when it would all end. Would I be able to handle the next trial? Then I read just the right verse during my morning devotional time. Jeremiah 31:13 stood out and gave me comfort. I recalled countless times when God gave me support and strength. Prayers from around the world covered me. Love held me up.

Hospice began twenty-four-hour crisis care for my mother to manage her pain and make her final time more comfortable. For years she had endured leukemia, diabetes, and various other health issues with little complaining. Fatigue limited her activities, but she learned to rest and do what she could. Pneumonia attacked her weakened body and put her into the hospital. Then she moved to a rehab center. Limited mobility required a wheelchair. Diseases wore out her frail body. She said she was ready to join my dad in heaven.

I longed for her to escape the pain. But her leaving intensified my other recent losses. Losing both parents would make me an orphan.

As mother lay near death months earlier, I listened and comforted my dad as we grieved. She rallied, but dad's health declined. When he died, Alan listened and comforted me as I cried.

When Alan faced death, I listened as he shared his struggles with me and cheered him as he endured a limited lifestyle. His joy in dying was a gift, but it didn't take away my sadness.

He said, "I don't know why you have had so much pain, but God has a plan."

Three of my biggest supporters could no longer comfort me or listen when I grieved. I cried alone. What was God's plan? Would normal ever return?

I remembered many years without major struggles. But even during my pain and grief, blessings appeared. Family, friends, and even strangers lifted me up. Each prayer, hug, and act of kindness gave me strength, hope, and encouragement for my extended journey of pain. God provided the comfort I needed. I pray often that I can also console others in their pain and grief. Without my own sorrow, I would not as easily recognize and understand their heartache.

Yahweh Yireh, one who sees the situation and provides for my needs, thank you for being with me in my grief. Amen.

Devo 19

My Easter Crosses

Most certainly I tell you, that you will weep and lament, but the world will rejoice. You will be sorrowful, but your sorrow will be turned into joy. (John 16:20 WEB)

No longer could I watch crosses form on the trees around our lake. For eight years, at our previous home, brown crosses rose on the pine trees every spring. Each year close to Easter, new growth at the end of the boughs produced amazing crosses.

At our new home, cypress trees lined the bank near the patio but no pines. I missed watching the crosses develop and reach toward heaven. I also yearned for the brightly colored mallards, white ducks, and turtles I watched at our other home.

Besides the difficulty of moving and leaving friends, death brought more losses. As we prepared to move, my dad died. A few months later my husband Alan passed away. Mother's lingering illness and impending death added to my grief. All three had been strong anchors for me. Tears appeared more often. Sadness stayed longer and grief held me tighter as I navigated my difficult journey without them.

The gospel accounts of Jesus' last night with His disciples and His betrayal revealed His own sadness. As He spent time with His followers in the garden of Gethsemane, He knew what was coming. *Then he said to them, "My soul is exceedingly sorrowful, even to death. Stay here, and watch with me." He went forward a little, fell on his face, and prayed, saying, "My Father, if it is possible, let this cup pass away from me; nevertheless, not what I desire, but what you desire."* (Matthew 26:38-3 WEB)

Those verses made me think of my own grief. I felt comforted knowing Jesus grieved too. He felt pain but was obedient. He knew there would be suffering for him but then joy would come. His home was not here but in heaven. Though my grief was consuming and heartbreaking at times, His example gave me encouragement and hope for the future.

In the fading light, I aimed my binoculars on the pine trees across the lake. Excitement filled me. Crosses pointed skyward. They were there all the time, but I had to search to find them.

Though different from my previous home, the landscape and wildlife offered a new outlook. From my new patio, turkeys paraded through my yard. Two large alligators visited the lake. A flock of cormorants and wood storks stayed for several weeks. Resident cardinals added color and chirping.

Life would never be the same. My journey through grief required me to search for moments of joy and embrace the changes. I'd continue to miss what I had lost, but I knew God would provide what I need for my new journey.

Father, lead me as I follow a new path. Help me find joy in the journey. Amen.

Devo 20

Good Friday?

Know this: my God will also fill every need you have according to His glorious riches in Jesus the Anointed, our Liberating King. So may our God and Father be glorified forever and ever. Amen. (Philippians 4: 19-20 VOICE)

As a child, Good Friday always puzzled me. Why was it called "good" when Jesus died? Over time, I learned and accepted that it was good that He died for our sins and then rose to go to heaven, but the name of that day still bothered me.

Then came Mother's death on Good Friday. How could her passing be good? How could I lose her after the recent deaths of Dad and Alan? I missed them all terribly. No longer could we chat, laugh, or visit. A lifetime of memories jammed my mind. She had prepared delicious meals for her family, friends, and fellow churchgoers. Even when confined to a bed, she worried about not being able to fix food for visitors. For many years she made her clothes and mine. She learned all types of crafts such as flower arranging, crocheting, and needlework. As a mother of three, she attended college to earn a degree to teach school. While teaching, she continued her education and received a master's degree. Her determination inspired me. Selfishly, I mourned as I remembered when she lived vibrantly with a healthy body.

Reality reminded me that her normal life ended years earlier when diseases robbed her of strength and energy. She tried to keep up with her normal activities, but gradually, her health declined. She slowed down for a while and then was forced to give up her favorite activities. For over a year at the end of her life, she lived away from her own home in the hospital, at a rehab center and finally, at my brother and sister-in-law's home. She longed for her former independent life with my dad. For three months we both faced a new normal without our spouses. A life not of our choosing.

After her passing on Good Friday, I looked ahead to the celebration of Easter. With a new body, she would be at home in heaven with Jesus. That was good!

At Mother's memorial service, Ashlyn, Emily, and I placed Easter lilies near her casket to symbolize the new home and bodies of Mother, Dad, and Alan. That was also good.

Father, thank you for your plan even when it doesn't make sense to me. Amen.

Devo 21

Mysterious Gifts

And Jesus looking upon them said to them, with men this is impossible; but with God all things are possible. (Matthew 19:26 ASV)

White roses, pink tulips, and white daisies decorated my home after Alan passed away. His wishes for me were coming true.

Over the years, Alan gave me roses, daisies, and other flowers. On my birthday soon after we met, he arrived at my house wearing a yellow shirt and clutching a dozen yellow roses. He realized I loved flowers of all kinds.

As he prepared for his death during the last two months of his life, a list of errands and duties stayed near him on the couch. Notify insurance company. Change names on accounts. Buy new car and bike for Rebecca. Show Rebecca important papers. Keep fresh flowers in the house.

We didn't find a florist in our new community. Bouquets we saw at the grocery store didn't satisfy him. Though we talked about flowers for the house, time ran out.

After his death, family members and friends sent several floral memorials and three rose bushes for my garden. His wish for me to have flowers came true.

Only a month after Alan died, I sent a bouquet of flowers to my mother for Valentine's Day. The first one after my dad's death.

The company offered a discount for a second order. I remembered Alan's desire for fresh flowers in the house, so I ordered a bouquet for myself. I scanned the calendar and randomly picked April 18 to have them delivered. But with so many responsibilities to attend to, I soon forgot about the order.

In April, after making arrangements for Mother's funeral, I faced a long, lonely drive home. Her death intensified my grief for Alan and Dad.

As I pulled into my drive, I noticed a long, rectangular box stood at my front door. Under the packing material, I found a dozen red, pink, and white roses. Their beauty made me smile. Even though April 18 was an arbitrary date to me, God knew the perfect day for me to receive the roses. Good Friday and the day of my mom's death.

As I gathered the wrappings and opened the enclosed envelope, my heart stopped. Through tears, I tried to make sense of the words.

Enjoy the day, Alan.

He never sent me flowers from an Internet company. I had given them my name, address, and e-mail address when I placed the order but didn't remember adding anything else.

Two spectacular gifts arrived that day. Even though I had forgotten about my purchase, God knew flowers would lighten the grief of Mother's death. The note reminded me of Alan's love and care. God orchestrated both mysterious miracles for a grieving widow and daughter.

Heavenly Father, thank you for supplying just what I need at the right time. Amen.

Devo 22

Gampa in Heaven

Children's children are the crown of old men; And the glory of children are their fathers. (Proverbs 17:6 ASV)

As the trustee of Mother and Dad's estate, in addition to being Alan's trustee, I faced another frustrating day dealing with all of the governmental bureaucracy. Difficult phone calls, copies of death certificates, and mounds of paperwork brought additional tears and more sadness.

I desperately needed a break from the daunting tasks. Since being with my young granddaughters always helped me forget the trials for a time and lifted my spirits, I decided to visit them. When I arrived at my son's home, Anne, Ashlyn, and Emily, sat at the dining room table, which held a pile of books and papers for their homeschool lessons. My job was to keep three-year-old Molly occupied while they studied. After each granddaughter wrapped me in a hug, Molly and I began her morning activities. First, she stretched rubber bands on a geoboard to match lower- and uppercase letters that her mom taped to it. Then Molly grabbed my hand and pulled me into the computer room to show me M on her computer program. After that, she rushed back to the living room. The trio working at the table grinned as I tried to run after her while she sped from one activity to another.

With no warning, she said, "I used to throw my stuffed animals at Gampa."

"What did he do?"

She giggled. "He threw them back."

"Grandpa was funny."

Her penetrating blue eyes met mine. "Gampa is still funny in heaven! He's telling jokes to Jesus."

When I miss Alan so much, I tend to forget he's now healthy, at home in heaven, and doing fine. But Molly didn't forget.

A few minutes later, she announced. "I love Gampa. I'll still love him when I'm in heaven."

Her random statements caught me off guard. Though adults often think children don't grasp the extent of death, at times my young granddaughter seemed to understand more than I did. Her childlike innocence and faith helped me deal with my losses.

She missed the buddy who played with her and made her laugh. However, her childlike belief and trust in God allowed her to accept his home in heaven. She talked about him no matter what she was doing. Though she could no longer play with him, her grandfather continued to be an important part of her life. I hope she never forgets.

Dear Lord, thank you for the innocence and faith of children. Help me learn to trust as they do. Amen.

Devo 23

Thriving Despite Afflictions

"Remain in me, and I in you. As the branch can't bear fruit by itself, unless it remains in the vine, so neither can you, unless you remain in me. I am the vine. You are the branches. He who remains in me, and I in him, the same bears much fruit, for apart from me you can do nothing." (John 15:4-5 WEB)

Bright pink flowers burst open. One, two, three, and — after a few days — fifteen blooms adorned the unidentified green plant.

Friends we met on a trip to Egypt several years ago had stopped to pray for Alan when they were visiting in our area. They also brought the plant to us. I transplanted it into a permanent pot and watered it as I did my other flowers. Several weeks after we received the gift, I watched in horror as every leaf dropped to the floor. The naked stems puzzled me. I changed its location and carefully fertilized it. When it moved it to a larger container with more space to grow, it toppled over. Nothing helped the mysterious plant or my disappointment.

One day at a local nursery, I noticed similar specimens covered in blooms. All were in small pots with roots protruding above the soil. To my surprise, the attached label said it was a desert rose. Determined to revive my pitiful plant, I followed instructions on the store label and repotted it into a smaller container. With more sunshine and only an occasional watering, my pathetic plant finally had what it needed. Healthy leaves sprouted and covered spindly branches. Tiny buds appeared and burst open with vibrant color. Each day more blooms emerged as it grew and flourished.

The plant I thought was dead gave me encouragement and beauty. With dry soil, hot sun, and minimum care, my desert rose thrived. And I discovered I, too, can survive in the face of rough conditions. Losing Alan, Mother, and Dad in such a short time felt overwhelming. The adverse conditions I faced seemed like an endless desert. Grief shrunk my world for a while. God often takes difficult conditions to help me grow and flourish too.

If God returns a spindly plant to life, how much more is He going to help me grow? The process won't be quick or easy. Some days I will have to search to see even a glimpse of growth. Other times there will be delightful developments. Multiple deaths permanently altered my life. Loneliness gripped me daily. Priorities changed. People grew more precious. Material items lost importance. Patience became my constant ally. Yet in all circumstances, God embraced me tightly.

When I gaze at my desert rose, I smile with understanding and hope. Even with unfavorable conditions, my desert rose and I can still bloom.

Creator, thank you for reviving my plant and me. When I am discouraged, I know you are with me. Amen.

Devo 24

Widow's First Anniversary Alone

Blessed are those who mourn, for they shall be comforted.
(Matthew 5:4 WEB)

He heals the broken in heart, and binds up their wounds.
(Psalm 147:3 WEB)

Tears blurred the words as I read the above verses from two of my daily devotionals. How could I celebrate a wedding anniversary when half of the partnership was missing and the survivor's heart was splintered?

The morning of our anniversary I sat quietly on my patio and watched the sun rise from behind the forest across the lake. Swatches of pink swept across the powder-blue sky. The spectacular sunrise lifted my eyes toward heaven. Could Alan see the breathtaking display? Did he know it was our ninth wedding anniversary?

As I remembered our life together, my tears gradually slowed and finally stopped. Even though I wished for more time together, we experienced wonderful years filled with travel, adventure, and blessings. Pleasurable times mingled with the difficult ones, which bonded us together, especially when his health deteriorated.

After we each experienced complicated life situations and years of being alone, God brought us together at a church dance.

Neither of us was looking for a mate, but we began dating and dating, for almost seven years. When we announced our engagement, we often heard, "It's about time."

As mature adults, we quickly adjusted to life together and overlooked minor annoyances and idiosyncrasies. Humor made the transition from being alone to being a couple easier. Alan encouraged me to be more adventuresome and took me places around the world I never imagined I would visit. When we met, his world consisted of work, the gym, and his home. I helped him discover the wonders of his local world.

We loved deeply. First God, each other, family members, friends, and many around the world that we met on mission trips. Love intertwined our lives and healed broken places from the past.

With more tears and laughter, I continued to remember our lives together. But I still longed to hold him one more time and feel his arms close around me. I ached to look into his blue eyes and hear him say, *I love you*. Despite my yearnings, I had to be content with years of extraordinary memories. Neither of us was looking for a spouse at the dance that night, but what a blessed surprise we received.

Father, thank you for the blessing of knowing Alan and being his wife. Amen.

Devo 25

A Granddaughter's Insight

And they were bringing unto him also their babes, that he should touch them: but when the disciples saw it, they rebuked them. But Jesus called them unto him, saying, "Suffer the little children to come unto me, and forbid them not: for to such belongeth the kingdom of God. Verily I say unto you, Whosoever shall not receive the kingdom of God as a little child, he shall in no wise enter therein." (Luke 18: 15-17 ASV)

Compassionate hazel eyes stared into my sad blue ones. Her gaze would not release me. My tears overflowed while small arms grabbed me and held tightly. Time after time during my journey of grief, Emily noticed my intense pain. Without a word, she would hold me in a secure hug. When my grief began, she was only seven years old, but even at that age, she noticed.

At Alan's memorial service, she and Ashlyn supported me as they held my hands for our walk down the long aisle. They gave me strength and courage. When tears trickled, Emily leaned against me and grabbed my hand.

Shortly after Alan's death, I accompanied my son, Chris, and his family to Williamsburg, Virginia.

One night as Emily came from the shower, she looked at me. "Grandma, what's wrong?"

"Nothing," I lied as tears tried to seep out.

"Grandma, *what is wrong?*"

"I miss Grandpa," I whispered.

She enfolded me in a hug, then I cried.

Another time, I had taken all three girls to church. Molly sat beside me with Emily and Ashlyn further down the row. The sermon, about how God uses difficult situations for good, made me think of those I had lost and how hard it had been. Emily glanced my way. I tried to look away so she wouldn't see my teary eyes. She kept staring and sensed my pain. She squeezed in next to Molly and wrapped me in her arms. Again, she held me while I sobbed.

Her sweet spirit senses my pain even when most adults don't. Although she is young, the Holy Spirit guides her, and she listens. She doesn't question, wonder, or hesitate. Normally, she says few words but immediately provides acts of comfort.

Her example, besides uplifting and supporting me, reminds me to do the same for others who are hurting. Instead of analyzing and pondering what to do, I should immediately obey the leading of the Holy Spirit as Emily does.

Heavenly Father, thank you for the compassion and insight of children. Help me to follow their examples. Amen.

Devo 26

Healing from Melon Balls

Why are you in despair, my soul? Why are you disturbed within me? Hope in God! For I shall still praise him, the saving help of my countenance, and my God. (Psalm 42:11WEB)

For several days, I couldn't shake my acute sadness. Grief seized me in a stranglehold. Tears flowed like a faucet that wouldn't shut off. Having lunch with members of my upcoming trip to the Holy Land seemed like a burden. How could I face new people with a smile when my crushed heart ached?

I opened the refrigerator. A shiny watermelon lurked inside and mocked me as I reached for it. With no enthusiasm at all, I placed it on the counter and sliced it in half.

For years, Alan and I formed a team to prepare watermelons. He always cut the juicy red fruit. Of course, we both sampled luscious bites while we talked and laughed. However, washing the dishes and cleaning up the sticky juice from the counter, and often the floor, was my job. I missed my watermelon partner terribly.

A faraway memory returned when I studied the green melon. Not long after we began dating, Alan invited me to his home for a brunch that he prepared. Colorful watermelon and cantaloupe balls filled a large bowl. A selection of bagels rested on his kitchen table. With full plates in front of us, we talked and gazed at the picturesque lake behind his house.

His artistic brunch presentation impressed me and led me to believe he enjoyed being in the kitchen. Later, I learned how limited his cooking skills actually were. We laughed about how he fooled me into thinking he was a master chef. Even without outstanding culinary skills, he captured my heart.

The memory of that day prodded me to rummage through my kitchen drawers. Finally, I located his melon ball maker. With each swipe across the ripe melon, memories swept over my grief. As the glass bowl filled with fruit, delightful memories filled empty places in my heart.

With my huge glass bowl of melon balls, I headed out to lunch. I reconnected with old friends and met new ones. A few others also grieved recent losses, so we bonded in our sadness. Prayers from the group enfolded us. By the time I left for home, my heart felt lighter. Grief lessened a bit. I looked forward to adventures on our trip with new friends and old ones.

Dear God, thank you for memories and new opportunities during times of grief. Amen.

Devo 27

What is Your Rose?

Then the King will tell those on his right hand, "Come, blessed of my Father, inherit the Kingdom prepared for you from the foundation of the world; for I was hungry, and you gave me food to eat. I was thirsty, and you gave me drink. I was a stranger, and you took me in. I was naked, and you clothed me. I was sick, and you visited me. I was in prison, and you came to me." The King will answer them, "Most certainly I tell you, because you did it to one of the least of these my brother, you did it to me." (Matthew 25:34-36, 40 WEB)

As the church service started, a red-and-white mint made its way down my row from one hand to the next. My friend Susie placed the candy, a gift from her son Steve, into my hand. Her somber face told me she knew why tears dribbled down my cheeks.

I unwrapped the candy as I had done hundreds of times. Its sweetness infused my mouth. Memories filled my mind. For many years before we left for church, Alan raided our candy dish. He grabbed at least two pieces, and often more, in case visitors sat near us. At the beginning of the service, he would hand me a treat. I'd give him a smile and my empty wrapper, which he put into his pocket.

55

Our little routine continued during his illness but ended with his death. Taking candy for myself wouldn't have been the same. The sweetness of my surprise candy reminded me of his thoughtfulness and love for me. It brought memories of our worship times together.

That evening Pastor Joel preached about looking for God in the ordinary circumstances of our lives. He related a story about a lady who received a rose from a stranger just when she needed it. After the service, I told Steve how Alan always gave me candy at church. Our ritual was a surprise to him. He said that he always kept mints in his pocket. With a smile and hug, he said, "That was your rose."

His simple gesture touched my heart. During my time of grief, God sightings have happened often, and I have received many special roses. I want God to open the eyes of my heart so I can also offer roses to others at just the right time.

Dear Father, thank you for my God sightings. Open my eyes and heart so I can be used by you. Amen.

Devo 28

Sunshine in the Grief

So support one another. Keep building each other up as you have been doing. (1 Thessalonians 5:11 VOICE)

For days I sorted through vintage pictures, old slides, and albums with wrinkled photos. Yellowed newspaper clippings, obituaries, and letters revealed interesting facts about my family's history. Some surprise revelations made me laugh and others made me cry. A few brought questions I longed to ask of departed loved ones. Secluded in my house with endless memories of those who had died, I plunged into deeper sorrow.

Numerous obituaries testified to the many losses of grandparents, uncles, aunts, and cousins. All left behind grieving loved ones. Until I faced the grief of losing immediate family members, I never really understood the extent of their losses. I realized that when deaths came, I didn't do enough to comfort those who were left behind.

To flee from my sorrow for a while, I decided to focus on someone else and visit a new friend in my neighborhood who was fighting her own battle. Because cancer severely attacked her body, she had recently entered hospice care. I wasn't prepared for the decline in her appearance since my previous visit. When I saw her pale, weak body cocooned in a hospital bed, grief slammed me with unwelcome memories of my parents in hospital beds during their last days. Oxygen tubes wrapped around her face reminded me of Alan's dependence on oxygen the last couple of months of his life. Her increasing frailty mirrored theirs and reminded me that her end was near too.

She immediately sensed my sadness and said, "Let me give you a hug."

I carefully put my arms around her so I would not cause her further pain. I apologized as I cried. I had gone there to cheer her up, but she offered me comfort in my grief.

From my patio that evening, I watched the sky gradually dim. Gentle rain peppered the lake as tears rushed down my cheeks. For days, I blocked them and tried to mask my grief. But built up emotions overflowed. At dusk that night, tears ran freely.

Thankfully, the peaceful lake scene calmed me. Surprise beams of sunlight glowed on the landscape across the water. A rainbow arch crowned the towering trees. Cardinals chirped their farewells. Frogs croaked and grasshoppers hummed. Throughout the entire day, God provided touches of healing to wrap around my grieving heart.

Father, thank you for providing a hug and kind words from a dying friend. Your magnificent creation also offered comfort and healing. Amen.

Devo 29

Reminders of Love and Compassion

Pure religion and undefiled before our God and Father is this, to visit the fatherless and widows in their affliction, and to keep oneself unspotted from the world. (James 1:27 ASV)

Each time I stepped onto my patio, the arrangements of plants, which formed an inside garden, took me back to special times with friends and family members. A flowering pink desert rose from traveling friends bloomed profusely. Vibrant amaryllis, obtained over twenty-five years ago from a neighbor's garden, waved their green leaves in the breeze. Purple wandering Jew, clipped from a friend's family legacy plant, cascaded from two filled pots.

Ten orchid plants congregated on a table in the corner. One was a neighbor's welcome gift at our previous home. A white orchid delivered along with a sympathetic hug, arrived from our realtor the day after my dad died. After moving to our new home, I divided my orchids into multiple pots.

Flourishing greenery filled four large decorative planters from family members and friends who comforted me after the deaths of my dad, Alan, and my mom. White, crimson, and pink rose bushes, given to me by loved ones, peeked at me from a memorial garden just outside my screened porch.

Each commemorative gift has contributed to my gathering of friends and family. At dawn when I meet God for spectacular sunrises, they join me. At dusk when I marvel at the beauty of the pink sky and serene lake, I am not alone but remember the love, compassion, and prayers of those who have supported me during good times and also the difficult ones.

Through the delicate flowers and towering trees, God reminds me that He cares for both the minute details and monumental situations in life. The rippling lake, joyful bird songs, and brilliant blue sky display the beauty of His creation. Rain, wind, and storms show His power.

My own grief has heightened my compassion for others who are also grieving. My plants remind me that personal touches, in various forms, continue to supply love and support.

Dear Lord, thank you for those who have surrounded me with love and kindness. Help me to do the same for others who are mourning. Amen.

Devo 30

Dark Clouds

In my distress I called on Yahweh, and cried to my God.
He heard my voice out of his temple. My cry before him
came into his ears. (Psalm 18:6 WEB)

Wind and rain thrashed against my windows. Red numbers on my clock screamed 4:30 a.m. The raging storm heightened my loneliness. Huddled under my warm, plush blanket, the turmoil within me matched the one roaring outside. Thankfully, within minutes the outside storm slowed and then stopped.

At dawn, I gazed at the horizon from my special spot on the patio. Gigantic gray puffballs rolled across the lightening sky. Rays of sunlight beamed like spotlights in the dark. Cool breezes wafted through the screen and made me shiver.

Despite the coolness, I decided to alter my normal schedule and take a bike ride through my neighborhood before doing my daily devotions. As I prepared to leave, the lake suddenly changed as thousands of raindrops pelted the still water. With my ride delayed, I began reading and praying. Clouds raced by and the sun quickly chased the rain away. My bike ride was on again. Before I even opened the garage door, a gust of wind abruptly brought another outburst of rain, an unusual occurrence for Florida.

An hour passed as I finished my devotional time. Sunlight illuminated the lake. Most dark clouds moved on. Butterflies and bees flitted from flower to flower. Dragonflies zoomed near the lake. Wind brushed leaves and rippled the water. The morning's activities alleviated some of my sadness at being alone. Later that morning, I rode my neon-pink bike through my neighborhood. Bike riders and walkers greeted me. Drivers waved. Warm breezes touched my face. Shady trees made the ride pleasant.

The dark clouds and sudden rains reminded me of ambushes of grief. Out of nowhere, they catch me off guard. Blast my peace. Erode contentment. Bring tears and isolate me. Mock my attempts to heal and overcome the pain. But like passing clouds, the ambushes abate for a while. Hope and joy return with the sunshine. The grief journey doesn't follow a predictable path forward but shifts up and down, backtracks, circles, and stalls. The trek continues with no apparent plan or direction. Over time, struggles become less painful and there are fewer cliffs to navigate. But the journey goes on and on and on.

Loving Father, thank you for holding me during my pain and distress. Thank you for your comfort as you lead me down the path of grief. Amen.

Devo 31

Unfocused and Jumbled

As for me, I will call on God. Yahweh will save me. Evening, morning, and at noon, I will cry out in distress. He will hear my voice. (Psalm 55:16-17 WEB)

Dirt clung to my fingers. My early-morning chore would help fulfill my required sixteen hours for the growing season as a member of the farm co-op. Two other members joined me in trying to plant the elusive teeny dots. It was almost impossible to pick up black bok choy seeds from little paper cups.

Rows of tall metal poles formed lines the length of the gardens. Four containers of soil were attached to each pole. Only by standing on my tiptoes could I see into the top tier. A seed was to go into every corner of the square hanging pots. I circled the suspended containers to make small indentations, drop seeds, and cover them with dirt.

My mind wandered. Did I get each corner? Had I remembered every pot? I tried to focus. I explored different, rather scattered, methods to help me plant the required seeds. Finally after several attempts, I established a routine. I made all the indentations. Then I dropped a seed into every hole and covered it right away. It worked. But by the time I figured it out, over half of my row was finished. I hoped I had not made mistakes on the first section.

Grief made much of my life unfocused and scattered too. Some days my mind functioned almost normally. Then the next day I felt confused and muddled. I heard not to make any important decisions for a year. That made sense to me but I wondered, would I ever be ready to make reasonable ones?

As I dealt with my parents' finances before and after their deaths—along with Alan's estate—phone calls, paperwork, and decisions overwhelmed me. There were days I felt as if I was drowning. I could barely lift my head to take a gulp of air. Over time, I learned to float or even paddle a bit. Then another wave hit. I felt myself get slammed to the bottom again. But the struggle to reach the top lessened in intensity and duration. Over and over family members, friends, and even kind strangers made my journey through the storms easier. As I floundered in my grief, they supported me. With eyes closed and uncertain of the path to safety, arms surrounded me and lifted me up.

Father, thank you for staying with me and providing unending help as I struggle to rise above the waves. Amen.

Devo 32

Compassionate Crocheting

Children's children are the crown of old men; the glory of children are their parents. (Proverbs 17: 6 WEB)

After filling a shopping cart with toys, eleven-year-old Ashlyn paid the clerk with her own money. "Shopping for five girls from the Dove Tree at church was way more fun than shopping for myself," she said.

After she learned to crochet the colorful scarves in her handicraft class at school, Ashlyn and I formed a small business so she could earn money before Christmas. I bought the yarn, then she paid me back from her profits. Her parents advertised her scarves on Facebook and delivered the completed creations. She worked diligently at home every day and even on her birthday train trip to Washington DC with her dad. None of us realized how many orders she would get. Her dad suspended orders for a while because she couldn't keep up.

At first, Ashlyn planned to donate half of her money to charity. As orders increased and the amount of money grew, though, she decided to use all of it to help others. She told us she didn't really want or need anything for herself. After reading many of the Dove Tree cards on the Christmas tree at her church, Ashlyn selected five girls and bought gifts they requested. Her excitement grew as she thought of their opening presents on Christmas morning as she always did with her family.

After the deadline for turning in the Dove Tree gifts passed, orders resumed as more and more people requested the lovely scarves. Ashlyn and her mom searched and searched for another ministry that helped children. When she saw Blessings for Babes, started by a family friend at church, she knew that was the one. The ministry helped couples who were adopting a child. She looked at pictures of the families and picked one who had a child in her younger sister's class. When she gave the adoptive mother a card with the monetary contribution, the mother cried. She was touched that Ashlyn would donate so much to their fund.

When orders overwhelmed her, Ashlyn taught me how to crochet the scarves so I could help fill some orders. Watching her work so hard encouraged me to reach out too. Christmas without Mother, Dad, and Alan wasn't easy, but focusing on others kept me busy and helped me deal with my pain. My granddaughter's selflessness and compassion not only blessed her recipients but also her grieving grandma.

Heavenly Father, thank you for the blessings that come from our grandchildren. Amen.

Devo 33

Sharing Comfort through the Pain

"We asked you to e-mail us your favorite verses," Pastor Vernon said.

I meant to send one in but forgot.

He continued, "We'll have time later for some of you to share your verses. Even though we know there are stories behind every verse, do not share the stories."

I grabbed my Bible. I knew the one I had to share. One microphone stood at the end of my row. I prayed I wouldn't cry, and a peace settled over me.

When Pastor Vernon asked for people to step to the microphones, I hurried to be first because I had to give my verse. As I stood, hundreds of eyes focused on me. I faced the congregation. "My verse is Joshua 1:9." The words of my Bible blurred. But knowing the verse in my heart allowed me to go on.

"This is my command: be strong and courageous. Never be afraid or discouraged because I am your God. I will remain with you wherever you go." I had to share a teeny part of my story. "Those were the last words my husband said to me before he went to be with Jesus."

Hands clasped mine as I returned to my seat. A lady near me wiped away tears. My chest thumped wildly. Tears squeezed out as I remembered my last night with Alan. After giving him his medication, I held his hand.

With bright but weary eyes, he told me that he loved me. He recited Joshua 1:9. Then he turned over and went to sleep. Four hours later I returned to give him more medication. He had removed his oxygen tube, fallen to the floor, and left me to be with Jesus.

My attention returned to Pastor Joel as he stepped on stage. "This is going to be a solemn sermon." He was right. He shared his own grief over the death of his son. More tears slipped down my face.

Three other widows sat by me. All of us still struggled with our losses. Pastor Joel looked at us several times. I felt he was speaking directly to our little group. "God doesn't always solve our problems. Sometimes something greater is coming," he continued. "We influence others by the way we turn to God in our pain."

I don't know why Alan and my parents weren't healed. But I have to look ahead to how God will use my pain. I overcame my fear of crying in front of the congregation because I wanted others to be encouraged. My pain enabled me to reach out and comfort those who were hurting. I prayed they would feel God enfold them in their intense pain and grief as He did for me.

Heavenly Father, thank you for your gift of the Word. In pain and suffering you comfort and encourage us with special blessings. Help me as I go forward. Amen.

Devo 34

Autumn Times

*And I heard a great voice out of the throne saying,
Behold, the tabernacle of God is with men, and he shall
dwell with them, and they shall be his peoples, and God
himself shall be with them, and be their God: and he shall
wipe away every tear from their eyes; and death shall be
no more; neither shall there be mourning, nor crying,
nor pain, any more: the first things are passed away.
And he that sitteth on the throne said, Behold, I make all
things new. And he saith, Write: for these words are
faithful and true.* (Revelation 21:3-5 ASV)

Spindly brown stalks of corn replaced the bright, thick foliage of
summer. Vibrant green bean fields were transformed into waves
of gold stretching on and on. Dazzling yellow and red leaves
glowed and dropped in the fall sunshine. Dramatic changes had
occurred between my July and September trips to Indiana.

Likewise, autumn changes appeared at my class reunion. Over
the years, much of the brown, blond, and black hair had turned
silver or gray. Agile, young bodies no longer jumped and ran
easily but creaked and slowed down. Bright eyes dimmed and
glasses appeared. Trim, healthy figures expanded outward and
shortened in height. Memories and stories flowed remembering

simpler, more carefree times. Laughter came with the recognition of aging faces and remembrances of high school silliness.

Many classmates knew of my year of losses. Tight embraces held me. Words of comfort and compassion blessed me. Tears trickled down weathered faces as we shared our heartaches and losses. Years of pain and struggles united us. No one bragged about important jobs or outstanding achievements. We shared life—both the good and bad. High school worries lost significance as real life happened. Carefree teenagers turned into caring, responsible adults.

For two days we reunited during meals, fellowship time, and riding on a float in the town's annual parade. Close friendships from long ago were reconnected and deepened. Life experiences broke down teenage barriers and allowed acquaintances to become friends. Unlike superficial exchanges during high school, many conversations included faith in God.

The class reunion, though difficult at times, took me further along on my grief journey. The support and understanding I received from classmates soothed the pain. Reconnections brought laughter and happiness. Old friendships intensified. Even though that weekend we all looked back at our past, we knew we had to move forward.

Dear Lord, thank you for reunions as we share life and comfort each other. Thank you for the blessings you gave in the past and those that will come. Amen.

Devo 35

Allowing Myself to Trust

He giveth power to the faint; and to them that have no might he increaseth strength. Even the youths shall faint and be weary, and the young men shall utterly fall: But they that wait upon the Lord shall renew their strength; they shall mount up with wings as eagles; they shall run, and not be weary; and they shall walk, and not faint. (Isaiah 40:29-3 KJV)

Anxious thoughts consumed me for several days and elevated my erratic blood pressure. Precautionary treatment for Lyme disease, after getting a tick bite, caused concern. Fatigue, nausea, and listlessness plagued me as I tried to prepare for my upcoming trip. Were my symptoms from Lyme disease or the medication to treat it? I could only think of how terrible I felt and wondered if I could even go on my cruise following the journeys of Paul along the Mediterranean with stops in the Holy Land.

Traveling overseas without Alan heightened my stress, since for years we traveled together around the world. I relied on him because he took care of all the details and made sure everything was in order. Intense loneliness and loss increased my tension. Sleep eluded me for several nights. I longed to crawl into a cocoon and wait for a metamorphosis.

But when friends responded to my plea for prayers, my days became a little brighter. A second doctor's visit relieved some of my concerns. My blood pressure eased downward. She stopped the strong medications for Lyme disease and gave me another prescription for my trip if symptoms appeared.

Gradually, my strength and optimism returned. Restless, sleepless nights improved. In the darkness before dawn, I prayed, *Take away my anxiety, Lord. You've taken care of me during all sorts of situations — divorce, moves, death, living alone, being a single parent, widowhood. Thank you. I trust you will continue to care for me as I take this trip. Amen.*

Instantly an answer came. *Finally. You're trusting Me again.*

The heavy weight from the previous week lifted. With a lightened heart, I looked forward to a magnificent journey to explore more lands of the Bible. With an improved attitude, I excitedly packed my suitcases and my compassion so I could embrace others and offer comfort to those who needed healing. I prayed to become closer to God as I journeyed through the holy sites.

Dear Lord, thank you for being my rock and support during hard times. Help me trust you and release my attempt to control. Open my heart and mind to your Spirit. Amen.

Devo 36

Dismal to Vibrant

Fear thou not, for I am with thee; be not dismayed, for I am thy God; I will strengthen thee; yea, I will help thee; yea, I will uphold thee with the right hand of my righteousness. (Isaiah 41:10 ASV)

Rain pounded the roof and dented the lake. Dark clouds shut off the morning sun. Wisps of fog swirled across the water. On my patio, I clutched a blanket around me and watched the dismal scene before me.

As I gazed at the lake, a variety of birds visited. A brilliant-scarlet cardinal hopped from branch to branch on the bare cypress. His dazzling color reminded me that God shows up even in the gloominess of life.

Nine cormorants fascinated me with their antics. Dark bodies, like overloaded boats, sank beneath the water so they looked like gliding cobras drifting across the lake. They dove for morning morsels, resurfaced, and shook their heads so breakfast could slide down their slender necks.

Like the red cardinal, the gleaming white egret didn't blend in with its surroundings. Its intense whiteness defied the dreariness of the day. Stepping along the shore, the egret circled the lake and stopped in front of my patio. After its elegant stroll, the stately bird hunched over like a feeble old man and waited. Then its neck stretched out like a long pipe, formed an S, and finally disappeared into its feathery body.

A smaller snowy egret flapped its wings vigorously. His flight took him up, down, and around the cormorants. He dove downward to the lake but aborted his landing inches from the water. After several failed landings, the persistent bird slammed into the water like a rocket. After a couple of seconds, his frenzied quest for food resumed. Though every bird belonged in the same environment, each one behaved differently.

I have discovered that dealing with grief is similar. The cause of my grief doesn't change, but how I handle it varies from day to day. Even minute to minute. Just when I think I have begun healing, unexpected tears and sadness come from a picture, a thought, a question, a song... Likewise, each person experiencing grief reacts in a unique way at a different pace.

Alan's last words to me remain etched in my mind. *Do not be afraid or discouraged. The Lord your God is with you always,* he had said. *I love you.* For weeks, he prepared me for his upcoming death. He had constantly assured me that God would take care of me when he was gone. He was right.

Heavenly Father, thank you for taking care of me in each situation I face. Amen.

Devo 37

Message from a Spider Web

Trust in the Lord with all your heart and lean not on your own understanding; in all your ways acknowledge Him, and He will make your paths straight. (Proverbs 3: 4-5 NIV)

Cause me to hear thy lovingkindness in the morning; For in thee do I trust: Cause me to know the way wherein I should walk; For I lift up my soul unto thee. (Psalm 143:8 ASV)

Sunlight glistened on long, thin strands that stretched from my roof to small bushes behind the house. Carefully crafted designs circled an intricate center as the spider plodded effortlessly about her two-foot web. The web fluttered in gentle breezes, but she ignored the wind and continued adding to her silky maze. Then, like a magician, she removed a large wedge of her complex creation, leaving no evidence at all of the willowy threads. She crawled around the large hole to the middle of the web and stopped. I checked on her frequently all day long, but she never moved from that one spot.

The following morning, I noticed she was in the same position. However, numerous holes distorted her embroidered pattern.

Despite the web disintegrating around her, she remained immobilized in the center of her handiwork.

When I looked for her on the fourth day, she was gone. Tattered remnants of her beautiful web flapped in the breeze. With sadness in my heart, I stared at the distorted mess and remembered the lacework of her lovely, painstaking design. Surprisingly, attached to the tangled remains, a few sturdy strands gleamed in the sunlight. Even though most of the web had been destroyed, strong anchors firmly held the remnants, preventing the web's complete collapse.

Some days my life mirrored the forlorn, scraggly web. Too many losses ripped out significant relationships and created huge voids. It seemed as if only a sticky jumble of a once happy, fulfilling life remained. But through all of my pain and grief, just like the spider web's anchors, God securely held onto me as I wobbled and sank. He never let me go even when my deteriorating life disintegrated around me.

With painstaking care, God is gently creating a different design from the shreds of my former life as He comforts and heals His broken and discouraged daughter.

Heavenly Father, take my hurt and make something new. Help me to use my pain to encourage and offer comfort to others. Amen.

Devo 38

Traveling the Bridge

I sought Jehovah, and he answered me, And delivered me from all my fears. (Psalm 34:4 ASV)

Fear crept over me each time I thought of the colossal bridge. As a child, I quivered as I stared down at the rushing waters of Tampa Bay when my dad drove across the mountain-sized bridge. The skyscraper-high structure could be seen for miles. At night it gleamed with a spectacular light display. Ships slid easily under its massive beams. Depressed souls leapt from its ledges.

In 1980, a freighter crashed into its beams and toppled part of the original bridge. That foggy morning, six cars, a truck, and a bus tumbled into the swirling water. Thirty-five people lost their lives in the tragedy.

Two years later, an open designed bridge replaced the enclosed, demolished one. An expansive view of Tampa Bay and the Gulf of Mexico delighted passengers. But for someone uneasy with heights, the view distracted and alarmed me.

I had a choice. I could drive over the frightening bridge or travel many miles farther through traffic and road construction to reach my friend's home. Neither option appealed to me.

Logic told me to choose the shorter but scary route. No cars had fallen off the new bridge into the deep waters of the bay. Over fifty thousand vehicles traveled over it each day. Surely, I wouldn't be the first.

I decided to look at the trip as an adventure instead of an obstacle. According to the map, the route made sense. Only in my mind did the journey become a problem. Since God walked with me during endless trials, I knew He would help me cross the terrifying bridge too. I began praying.

At the tollbooth, drops splattered my windshield. Adding rain to an already nerve-racking drive made it even more horrifying. However, after a few miles, the rain stopped. All around me, cars whizzed by. I glanced out at Tampa Bay to my right and the Gulf of Mexico on my left. No one slowed as they approached the ascent from the causeway.

Gradually, my car rose above the blue waters. Sunlight broke through the clouds. I could only glance at the incredible panorama that stretched for miles and miles.

As I crested the peak, I yelled, "I made it!!"

The descent exhilarated me. Waves glistened and miniature boats bobbed in the azure water. What relief to overcome a major fear.

For over two years, life presented me with innumerable fears and obstacles. I faced them and went on because I had no other acceptable option. For a time, fear of the bridge escalated and robbed me of peace and contentment. Scaling the Skyway reminded me that I don't travel alone.

Loving Father, thank you for taking my hand and leading me through my trials. Amen.

Devo 39

Don't Forget

Fear thou not, for I am with thee; be not dismayed, for I am thy God; I will strengthen thee; yea, I will help thee; yea, I will uphold thee with the right hand of my righteousness. (Isaiah 41:1 ASV)

Loneliness set in as I tried to reduce my never-ending list of phone calls, paperwork, and other unwelcome tasks. During a break in my mundane chores, planting yellow and purple flowers in my garden revived me. Unfortunately, when I went inside, the house felt as hot as the temperature outside. The air conditioner wasn't blowing out cool air. An almost-new air conditioner should not have broken—especially on a holiday weekend. I called a repair service and then waited all day long for someone to come. Since Alan had always taken care of our repairs, I felt helpless and unqualified.

Finally, a repairman arrived around 7 p.m. As soon as I told him the problem, he moved to the outside unit and got to work. I kept slyly peeking out my office window. One side of the unit lay on the ground next to a jumble of parts. As dusk set in, I ventured outside to see what he could tell me. But he was gone. At first, I thought he went home and left me with a puzzle of components on the ground. But I found him working on the unit in the garage.

He told me he was trying to temporarily fix the problem since the broken piece had to be ordered.

"I feel badly that you had to be here so long," I said. "Especially on a Friday."

Sweat drenched his shirt. "I feel badly that you're hot." His determination to fix the situation for me made it not quite so bad.

After seeing the repair truck by my house, a neighbor called to see if I needed anything. She offered a room where I could be cool for the night. Anne, called to see if I wanted to come to their house. Two other friends said I could stay at their homes. But by that time of night, I didn't feel like leaving, so with several fans and the makeshift repair job, I remained cool for the night.

When I prayed later that evening, I heard God say, *I'll take care of you*. Tears streamed down my face. Why did I keep forgetting? Though I no longer had the security, companionship, and presence of Alan, I was not alone.

God surprised me multiple times that day. A kind repairman showed up. Friends and family members offered help. Flowers rejuvenated me. Sunshine sparkled on the lake. Alan's picture smiled at me. God blessed me and continues to comfort me. My life changed when Alan died, but God didn't.

Father, your presence comforts and holds me up. Even in my sadness, you remain faithful. Amen.

Devo 40

Tender Birthday Memories

Thou hast turned for me my mourning into dancing: thou hast put off my sackcloth, and girded me with gladness; to the end that my glory may sing praise to thee, and not be silent. O Lord my God, I will give thanks unto thee forever. (Psalm 30:11-1 KJV)

Last year, Alan and I celebrated my birthday together. Even though he was gone, remembrances of that memorable day surged through my mind. Because of his declining health, he rested all day so he could take me to a special restaurant. When I gently told him we didn't have to go, he said, "I want to do it." Although we didn't say it, we both knew it would probably be the last birthday we celebrated together.

A couple of months earlier, I took over driving because it was too exhausting for him. With no handicapped spaces available near the restaurant that evening, I dropped him off at the curb in front of the restaurant. Tears threatened as I circled the area searching for a parking spot. As I walked alone through the dark, I thought of the years Alan took care of me but recently our roles had reversed. Neither of us liked the changes, but we learned to adapt. The nagging question in my mind kept coming back. *Will this be my last birthday with Alan?*

He carried his oxygen tank as we walked into the darkened dining room. At our table for two, glittery birthday confetti sparkled on the black tablecloth next to a simple white card with our name printed on it. The special touches welcomed us and made me smile. I forced the intruding question away.

Our attentive waiter explained the menu and answered questions. Alan and I talked quietly and waited for our meal. Only a few diners sat nearby in the small, elegant dining room. No one else knew this would be our only visit together to the award-winning restaurant.

We savored every delectable bite of each creatively decorated dish. Normally, we skipped dessert, but Alan urged me to choose one for our special occasion. He declined to order one for himself but took a bite of my luscious crème brûlée. We enjoyed every bit of our sumptuous meal. Throughout the evening, his oxygen tank, taken there as a precaution, remained unused on the floor. His taste buds, recently dulled by medications, allowed him to appreciate each bite that night. For one evening, we shoved aside thoughts of his impending death and enjoyed my birthday celebration. As I remember special birthday memories with Alan, I merge them with new ones made since his death.

Dear Lord, thank you for the years with Alan and new opportunities ahead. Amen.

ABOUT THE AUTHOR

Rebecca, a retired teacher, lives on a peaceful lake in Ce itral Florida. She and her husband Alan traveled on mission and pleasure trips around the world to every continent. Inspiration for her writings have come from travel, nature, her granddaughters, and life events.

She has won awards from Word Weavers, a Christian writers organization. Her writings have been included in several anthologies such as More Christmas Moments and Celebrating Christmas with …Memories, Poetry, and Good Food. Articles have appeared in publications like Focus on the Family's Adventure in Odyssey's Clubhouse magazine and Lake Forest Living.

Her life changed dramatically with the deaths of her parents and husband, but with God's help she is adjusting to her new life. Follow Rebecca on her blog at rebeccacarpenter.blogspot.com.